CULTURED FOR

GROWTH

OTHER BOOKS BY S. P. SCOTT

Orchids and Roses

Visions From My Father

The Day the Bow Breaks

CULTURED FOR
GROWTH

How the right culture can reignite a congregation

for growth and spiritual development.

S. P. Scott

ISBN: 978-969-41-9237-6

ISBN: 978-969-41-9238-3

Published by S. P. Scott

Printed in United States

First Printing: January, 2024

CONTENTS

ACKNOWLEDGEMENTS

This book is dedicated to all the people who have mentored, coached, prayed for, and encouraged me. Special acknowledgement to my previous and current church leaders and pastors who have mirrored biblical principles and have endeavoured to create a church culture that is conducive to personal growth and a sense of belonging.

You have all contributed to me being moulded into a leader, and it is from these experiences that I can share some of the contents of this book.

One thing stands out during this journey: leading or engaging in the absence of compassion and intentionality is akin to escorting someone in through the front door only to disregard them as they walk out the back.

To my remarkable son, Ruel and daughter, Jayda – two amazingly gifted and talented children, both with an incredible future lying ahead of them ... in whom I pray His truth will embed, and that it will endure to their children's children – and even beyond their generation.

INTRODUCTION

I love a dinner party. Not that I am a great cook – but I have faith that the desired scent, flavour, and texture will be achieved with the right ingredients. Like a skilled chef, the host or the catering team sets out intentionally to obtain the several necessary items to achieve the desired outcome. They are conscious and determined to ensure their guests will begin to salivate long before the first aesthetically appealing dish is placed on the perfectly laid out table, then anxiously tuck into what their eyes promised to be a sumptuous meal.

Over thirty years ago, I responded to one such invitation. Since then, I have continually invited others to come and dine. Time and again, we, the ecclesia, enact the mandate of spreading the Good News of the gospel in various forms, with the intention that people will accept the invitation and believe in Jesus Christ. Of course, if for whatever reason they are unable to be a part of our church family, we say, 'it is ok' - but ultimately, we would very much like for them to become a member of our congregation.

And for the most part, they do.

The question is – what are some of the key ingredients necessary to cause someone who has tasted the beautifully presented meal to stay and dine, as opposed to concluding the flavour is off, the texture is wrong, and the company ... leaves even more, to be desired?

In Cultured for Growth – I will seek to explore not only the beauty of the worship service or the myriad fellowship events but, more so – the quality of what is taught and the company in which the learning for growth and development takes place.

I acknowledge this is not original, being drawn somewhat on the work and testimony of others... but I believe there is much more to be said, and it is essential that it is explored. Particularly as we seek to understand and learn the lessons from the pandemic, which brings us face to face with the post-COVID-19 terrain, we must now traverse.

See you on the next page ...

The Author.

CHAPTER 1

THE CONTEXT

What they said: feedback from conversations

As a child, the cultured person was unmissable. Back in those days, I did not know how to define it, but I could easily describe what I saw. It was an almost organic way of being; certain characteristics were exhibited among Christians as they interacted with each other and the world. However, in recent times – sadly, it has been demonstrated less frequently among believers. This has led me to conclude that there is but a cultured remnant and the world is at risk of losing a cultured church, which I am tempted to think is much to their pleasure.

Post-pandemic, the risk could be thought of as elevated, and this is due to new practices which have been observed among Christians, practices one would deem perilous. Until recently, I was unfamiliar with the use of the term - 'outside the four walls' as it relates to born-again evangelical Christians. This practice became apparent when, due to a recent change in my role, I began to engage with a wider cross-section of people - increasingly, more people have been noted to use the term to describe their new preferred place of worship. Conscious of Hebrews 10:25, where the Lord commands us to meet and not to forsake the assembling of ourselves together, I became uncomfortable as the conversations developed. Respected Baptist minister and political scientist Ryan Burge, in his book, *The Nones: Where They Came from, Who They Are, And Where They Are Going*, states that "church attendance is the first thing that goes, then belonging, and finally – belief. In that order."

With an acute awareness of a report by The Tearfund (2020) that shows in the United Kingdom (UK), the ratio of women to men in church as 65% to 35%, concern quickly accompanied the growing discomfort. Not only because, over the last 3 years, I have assumed, for the first time, the presidency of our local women's ministry, but as a mother to two teenagers of the opposite sex, a 15-year-old girl and a 17year old boy, curiously I wondered what would be unearthed, should that and similar data be interrogated.

Other surveys confirmed what anecdotal evidence predicted; the ratio of women to men seeking to worship outside the four walls is remarkably higher. Importantly, it flagged an increasing number of young people across sexes are of a similar persuasion. While it would be easy to share my perspective and information gleaned from further afield, I thought it would be more valuable to understand this new wave (or resurgence) pertaining to my immediate context. I am also mindful of my values and personal and denominational biases, and therefore, it was necessary to review and present what others have highlighted as their experiences that could have contributed to the risk.

Consideration was also given to my role as an inexperienced parent to two teenagers seeking to understand young people and their relationship with the church community. My new role heading the local women's ministries made me think of the women I serve, those I seek to engage with, and what this new phenomenon means as it relates to their post-pandemic faith walk expectations. Generally, I thought it important to understand the reason (s) behind this cult-like behaviour, whose aim appears to mimic a pandemic in scope and no doubt also affects our men.

Although by no means extensive, several voices ... other than a lone one, are more of a representative sample from which to start what should hopefully be meaningful conversations. This led me to embark on a year-long, informal research that included conversations with over one hundred randomly selected people of various demographics, all of whom identify as 'born again Christians'. Some no longer attend church, others have moved on to join other congregations, while several have chosen to visit 'as and when', with no commitment to a specific congregation eminent.

All participants engaged freely. Neither the name of each person's previous church nor the individual's country of birth was requested - or offered. However, age and gender were noted. It was concluded that, while the latter mattered from the point of view that male and female, as well as the youth and older adults, have notable roles as expressed in scripture, conversely, information relating to the former is of no scriptural basis and, therefore, was not solicited. It is also recognised that despite socio-cultural differences, there are commonalities within sex and age groups, which makes the fundamental question of how we can create a contributory environment and encourage everyone (both inter and intra-demographic) to exhibit the same Kingdom culture practices a pertinent constant.

It was unanimously agreed that numerous changes have occurred over the years and that it is difficult to engage with an environment and not affect or be affected by it. Some highlighted what they refer to as stark and profoundly radical differences in our society and church community but also admitted there are some things unchanged.

The function of the church over generations has been uncontested. Its recognition as a vital part of the community in providing 'cradle-to-grave' activities and support for everyone was echoed. As key places of comfort and refuge in times of crisis, offering a lifeline and socialisation to individuals and communities was repeated. It was also agreed that participation in the church community is hailed as having a direct correlation with increased generosity, better standard of living, improved health outcomes and longer life.

The church community is helpful in creating and maintaining more stable families and improved community cohesion - all of which are important to the wellbeing of any nation. This view mirrors previous studies done in the United States (USA) that have found a positive association between church attendance and a reduction in suicide tendencies, depression, and benefits to cognitive function in older people.

In fact, in the United Kingdom (UK), local Councils, as well as organisations within the voluntary sector that serve local communities, highlight the need for partnership with the church due to increased complaints of loneliness and its corresponding effects on one's mental health which is a major concern.

Key findings of the Savanta opinion poll, which surveyed 2061 UK adults online between the 9th and 12th December 2022, call attention to:

- Three-quarters (75%) of UK adults agree that churches, chapels, and meeting houses are important for society as they provide a space for activities and support for local people, such as foodbanks and warm spaces.

- A large majority of UK adults (73%) also agree that the UK's churches, chapels, and meeting houses are an important part of the UK's heritage and history (nationalchurchestrust.org).

Buoyed by most of the above, it is important to bear in mind that the church's sole purpose is not as the healer of the world's social ills.

Stanford anthropologist and the author of When God Talks Back: Understanding the American Evangelical Relationship with God, Professor Tanya Luhrmann, states, 'What one might call an avalanche of medical data has demonstrated that, for reasons still poorly understood, those who attend church and believe in God are healthier and happier and live longer than those who do not.' Luhrmann has focused primarily on Evangelical Christians in her studies and has dismissed what other researchers have theorised to conclude that it's not just the benefits of social networking that makes churchgoers happy. Luhrmann believes that those who were able to experience a loving God vividly were healthier – "leads to better health and when God was experienced as close and intimate, the more someone prayed, the less ill the person was".

There is still another and possibly more vital function of the church, which goes beyond its creative and varied programming and the architecture of the places in which we gather, and that is, all congregations should have not only evangelism, but equally discipleship at its heart.

However, like so many spaces where people come together for a shared purpose, the church is not immune to external influences and pressures. Therefore, it too, has had to acknowledge the political, economic, social, technological, legal, and environmental challenges; unfortunately, many congregations have not been left unscathed by the pandemic and continue to bemoan the steep reduction in attendance post-lockdown. While happy to see those who have returned, there is the acknowledgement that not only is there a substantial change in numbers, but the demographic looks quite different too.

No doubt there is a discourse underway among faith groups, and at various levels of many organisations across the globe as 'the reset' continues and people... particularly leaders, seek to learn the lessons from the pandemic.

Like a disease process, for symptoms to appear in any given circumstance, there is always a root cause. And this is true for both favourable outcomes such as those mentioned by Luhrmann, numerous other studies, and National Churches

Trust. And this is true for those unfavourable outcomes, which all efforts have been made to prevent.

Responders had, on average, three points, which they passionately relayed. Each responder was placed in one of three categories from which their responses were analysed.

i.   Unaffected physically by Covid-19 (as if never had the virus)

ii.   Affected but made a full recovery

iii.   Continues to have symptoms.

Responders' opinions on both the pre- and post-COVID environments were also analysed.

It is foolhardy to not recognise that many people are left traumatised by COVID-19. For some, it was a near-death experience never to be forgotten, as the starkness of their mortality led to – in addition to other things – an overwhelming desire to live what number of days they have remaining in a wholesome, happy, and productive way.

Those living with its physical effects are categorised as having 'Long Covid'. And although the mental challenges are usually less obvious than the physical – they are no less sinister, as both demand the individual's mitigation skills daily.

Symptoms range from memory lapse to brain fog, persistent tiredness and insomnia. Difficulty sleeping, chest pain, chest tightness, the loss of ability to smell, muscle aches, depression, and anxiety – are some of the conditions on which decisions are taken and the context in which life is lived for many people.

Among the responders, less than 10% confessed to this being their reality and why they will remain in the 'periodic visitors' category. For almost 25% who have been physiologically touched by COVID but have managed to make a full recovery they have voiced having less patience for what they saw as the struggle for control and power or the need to be accommodating of that which does nothing for their mental or general health and wellbeing. They concluded their spiritual welfare could be met from the comfort of their couch and opted for yet another service on demand.

The remainder denied any physical or psychological effects but agreed with others, that the type of activities on offer and the absence of some ranked high on their list of frustrations. This was followed closely by the need for inspiration and 'fulfilment'. There were mixed views on the teaching of the

Scriptures, as some bemoaned what they concluded were inconsistent Bible study sessions, and when they did occur, the content was woefully inadequate.

Others felt disempowered - thought there was little to no opportunity to express their feelings or contribute outside of giving tithes and offerings. They stated that the absence of a voice made them feel undervalued and unappreciated. For those under 30, 'omitted' was the word used to express how they felt. In their view, the activities, such as weekly services, targeted the older members and in their minds, they were of no significance, or they could not relate... it's boring – 'dead'.

On the other hand, some older adults felt overlooked – forgotten and referred to it as 'the young people's show'. That they are no longer of value was a shared sentiment. In the words of a nearly eighty-year-old senior, "People of my age don't count".

Ministry and activities geared towards families and those with children were commended; however, some singles said they felt marginalised, while the widows and widowers saw themselves as outsiders. A few persons spoke of the need to feel seen in the presence of their hidden disability, which neither of them said they felt safe to disclose to fellow brethren. Some parents felt children and young people with disabilities must be recognised and included and not be told or made to feel - they are possessed by a demon.

Almost all responders mentioned some members' 'harsh – challenging – unacceptable' behaviour. The lack of decision-making and absence of corrective measures for known recalcitrant members were also featured.

Descriptors such as imbalance, 'part of Pastor's in-crowd'... cleeks, silos, to stronger adjectives such as dysfunctional, entered the descriptive discourse. Some feel there should be a 'no respecter of persons' approach and that the days when the men of the cloth are held in such high regard are ending - baring a few who, to them, have not yet defiled their garment of integrity and unfortunately have been labelled alongside the perpetrators.

Lack of regard for the pulpit - moral corruption bullying, are some of the even more sobering descriptors.

Passive-aggressive behaviour, particularly when unable to undertake a certain request or task - when one is made to feel guilty and judged as 'not putting God first'.

Primarily among the under 40-year-olds, the question of gender equity was flagged. And some have voiced frustration at the lack of clarity as they seek an answer to the practice which continues to dominate some churches, where the pastor or those in leadership 'must be a man'. Some people vehemently disagree with the principle generated by that collection of words as the conversation around female leadership and the church rages on with no sign of abating or a consensus any time soon.

Across demographics, there is the recognition of the 'freedom to speak up' phenomenon, and in this era of 'telling your story', many think there should be no reservation in sharing or being vulnerable - in what they see as a 'new dawn' for the church. However, it is expected that this 'new dawn' should not include limiting someone's feelings to the 'pray about it' or 'leave it to God' section, to which it is usually relegated - if at all recognised. It is clear from a few that suffering in silence can no longer be an option. In their view, although less frequently so, mental instability affects those who are of the faith, and the lack of compassion and empathy breaks their heart in equal measure or ...more, due to the sheer unexpectedness of it – if not, simply the disappointment.

For them, talking about their experiences, particularly at a time when many organisations outside of the church community continue to encourage others to do so, helps to validate what would otherwise not have been spoken of. It also offers an outlet, which to them is sometimes cathartic and other times empowering. For example, someone who has lived in a domestic violence household for over 30 years and remained silent in the church insists this needs to be called out and destigmatised. Mental wellness and a holistic approach to church are high on the list of things brought to the fore.

Respondents felt that financial illiteracy or the lack of a viable economic plan or financial strategy for some churches is unnecessary and wreaks of poor stewardship. They need a robust plan that does not include a frequent request for money from brethren, who are all encountering financial hardship - some of whom, sadly, have since been made redundant and yet to regain their pre-COVID financial freedom.

Others wonder why there seems to be an either-or relationship between intellectualism and spiritualism and yearn to see them both co-exist without the judgement of pride and accusations of lack of humility in the presence of the former.

Some singles feel the church needs to understand and address the challenges they face, particularly in the changing demographic landscape and that it should hold more frank conversations around the practicalities of living with singleness while hoping to be married. Many young women voiced feeling 'unprepared' for marriage and insist this should be taught by the church outside of the limited time given to pre-marital counselling. Others feel there is still a lack of clarity around divorce and remarriage.

They spoke of the church's position around topics such as artificial insemination in the case of someone who is unmarried and nearing the end of their childbearing age, being unclear, and will there be a single view on tattoos.

For a few, on the background of God so love the world that He gave His only begotten Son, forgiveness should follow the understanding that all sin (except blasphemy) is pardonable - therefore, someone who has assumed a new gender - transitioned - who is now born again and wishes to be married to someone who is opposite to the current gender, that choice should remain unquestionable.

The post-Covid environment is one where some voiced feeling 'tired' and, therefore, it is too late to care about the thoughts and subsequent behaviours of others. The narrative of 'out of touch' seems to pervade the external environment as people increasingly begin to tell their stories and share their lived experiences. For many, 'unsympathetic' and 'lacking compassion' featured prominently. Although some identified it, it was observed as not extended to all - a perceived disparity which gives rise to complaints of bias and partiality.

The conversation about the church being a hospital got louder, not because it is any longer seen as a place where people go to get well, but more of a place where the sick and injured are either left to deteriorate, or the well becomes unwell. All the while, the underlying cause goes undiagnosed, either because physicians are unsure of interventions and, therefore, feel powerless or are oblivious to the symptoms.

Notably, over 70% of responders mentioned how they - 'feel'. And while these are individuals' perceptions, and not all are factual statements, nonetheless, each statement highlights how these individuals regard, interpret, and understand the context and recalls two common sayings: one coined by John Maxwell, "People don't care how much you know until they know how much you care." While the legendary Maya Angelou compliments that with, "People will forget what you said, people will forget what you did, but people will never forget how you made them – feel."

And this is what rings out the loudest in this new era. That mantra of - being in touch with one's feelings. Moving away from what disturbs one's peace. Individuals voiced being keen to shun whatever is perceived as toxic environments and places that cause discomfort.

So, pre-COVID - we see where, like an addict, it appeared congregants felt they had to attend that church or else... and some have yet to decide if churchgoing for them was merely a habit. If so, what could have been done, if anything - to have assisted the move from ritual to real transformation?

Today, is there a post covid reckoning – where we must now face the decisions made by those who went through a form of 'detox' during lockdown and have come out cleansed of what they felt was something they needed to get out of their blood and out of their minds. People who have taken that bold step to venture elsewhere or, sadly, to move away from the command to assemble ourselves together, to remain outside the four walls.

Personal Notes and Reflections

What mentioned in Chapter 1 that I can relate to?	Is there anything I have observed that I could add?	What is my view about – The Context.	Any other comments

CHAPTER 2

HOW DID WE GET HERE

The Diet of the Uncultured

L ike many things, this is not an acute occurrence. It evolves – insidiously.

As a result of the pandemic, we realise what is known to be true: people do not very often think consciously about their actions. However, during times of uncertainty such as the pandemic or – even in the case of a change of pastor or leader, there is an increase in thought about previously unconsidered practices. This intentionality of thought brings certain matters to the forefront of one's mind, to a level of consciousness which prompts or drives the individual to reconsider the status quo and, if necessary, to act.

A review of the National Census for England and Wales over the last 3 decades shows an increase in the number of voluntary responses to the religion question from 92.9% (52.1 million) in 2011 to 94.0% or 56.0 million in 2021. However, over the same period, there was a decrease in the number of people who identify as Christians.

In 2001, 71.7% identified as 'Christian'; ten years later, in 2011, that percentage was reduced to 59.3% and in 2021, for the first time, less than half the population (46.1%) described themselves as Christians. This coincided with an increase in the number of people reporting "No religion" to 37.2% (22.2 million) in 2021 from 25.2% (14.1 million) in 2011. Again, this continues the trend between 2001 and 2011, when the number of people reporting "No religion" had risen from 14.8% (7.7 million people).

According to the National Churches Trust's April 2019 data, there were approximately 40300 churches in the United Kingdom, over 1000 more than pubs and of this number, 1500 were Pentecostal churches, 1400 smaller denominations and 1300 referred to as 'new churches. A poll by the same organisation in 2022 cited that number as 39000. The average age of those who identified as "Christian" increased from 45 years in 2011 to 51 in 2021. 8 out of 10 people 80 years and over identified as practising Christians, while you are most likely to find non-believers in groups of those 30-year-olds and below, where more than half do not believe in any god – 'the NONES'.

From the above, we can see the change in composition could be due to many contributing factors, such as differing patterns of ageing – the ageing population has been widely documented. The personal choice regarding fertility may have contributed to changes in mortality rate and migration. Changes may also be caused by differences in how individuals chose to answer the religion question between censuses, a practice which in academic circles earned the name "social desirability bias", where people may have chosen to answer inaccurately on surveys.

The quest to make sense of the above is not new; neither has it been undertaken by a mere few. Over the years, many different sets of data have been published, and they vary in number investigated, time periods and demographics... covering many Christian organisations.

Christianitytoday.com points to a survey of 1,164 protestant pastors, followed by 17 focus groups and 9 in-person case studies, which found what they concluded as varied and complex explanations: from health concerns to other disagreements – to even ... a feeling of betrayal. And I am sure you can point to other challenges in your experience that could have contributed to the 'context' described.

Admittedly, the world is becoming more secular. That is, it seeks to interpret life based on principles derived solely from the material world, without recourse to religion or God the creator. Therefore, the focus is towards "temporal" and material concerns. The church has an authentic organic nature – the New Testament knows no other kind of church, and it continues to interact with its surroundings to reciprocate influences with its contexts, which leads to changes as contexts determine.

As the secular and the sacred engage, internal and external factors collide to influence the forms of expression of the church, from the mode of dress, for example, to our language. And many theologians continue to analyse and reconstruct what they assume the face of the church will look like over time.

For many, the question remains: What tendencies can be identified that will influence the future face of the church as sin, in particular, pride, continues to feed this post-secular mindset?

Turning the focus internally, could it be a failure to make disciples, and if so, is it that we do not have sufficient theological reasons to want to spread our faith? Theology influences behaviour, and there is evidence of a substantial theological drift over time, particularly in some older or traditional churches, while some of our 'modern' churches appear to have a near-truth 'post-modern' version of the Bible. They present a one-sided version of our Creator. They cite God as a patient God of love who bestows bountiful blessings only, with little to no balance with Him as The Holy, Eternal, Sovereign God who is returning as The Righteous Judge. A balanced gospel is necessary for people to know who they worship and what He expects.

The former was a point raised by several respondents in the over one hundred people interviewed as they highlighted concern around the absence of meaningful Bible study sessions. There was a particular mention of the focus being so much on the praise and worship experience followed closely by a very demonstrative preaching session; however, – astonishingly- no time for Sunday school in a culture where children are increasingly more unruly and ungodly – as many are from homes where God is not recognised or if He is, He is not prioritised. This appears to be one of the underlying factors contributing to the growing number and diversity of NONES (people primarily under 30 years old having no belief in any god).

With the advent of social media, which is undeniably incredibly far-reaching in scale and scope... and so too, the spread of truth and mistrust in an unequal measure, favouring the latter – with more airtime seemingly given to the dissemination of incorrect information about the Bible. This presents a challenge to all denominations. There is a challenge to evangelicals also:

Does the population of evangelical churches know what they are meant to believe – is there consistency in messaging?

Is there a common view and conviction regarding the realities of hell and heaven?

Is there a consensus around what salvation is and how to receive it?

Is everyone having the same experience in their respective church community and in their individual faith walk?

Have we mistaken church attendance for growth and maturity – by being happy with 6 to 60 or 50 to 100 as a sense of accomplishment and status symbol resulting in apathy?

Is there a passivity to the lack of sound doctrine, the absence of a distinct feature in our spiritual attire and complex language type?

Is there a preoccupation with activities which unintentionally breeds an accompanying negative way of 'how things are done around here'?

Is the church so busy meeting the needs of the community that the needs of the congregation, such as family time and wellbeing, hang in the balance or is it the other way around?

Could it be that some leaders are caught up with sentimentalism to certain practices founded in hand-me-down beliefs and a deep reverence for church history, to the detriment of a refusal to explore and have a nuanced review of how things are done – have those engrained beliefs been tested against what the Bible says?

Is it the aim to intentionally hear what God is saying to the church today?

Are leaders kept abreast of the changing needs both internally and externally and are therefore able to either act proactively, respond or both?

Do leaders hold a sense of entitlement and a high level of self-importance, which give rise to a hands-off, nigh-on, unapproachable, aloof disposition – out of touch ... meeting the needs of a few as they ignore the whole?

Are some leaders paralysed by an aversion to 'risk' alongside a preached faith walk?

Are there some who are quite tolerant of discrimination and mediocrity, while others remain suspicious of outside voices?

Is it that we are oblivious to the effects of our proximity to the world, or is there a deliberate and conscious coupling in certain parts of Christendom which, like the yeast working its way and spreading its tentacles through the whole dough – are we feeding from that – dough?

Has the world figured out our kryptonite ... noting the many of us who have moved away from our Kingdom heritage and cultural practices to embrace religious norms and rituals – only to possess a form of godliness?

Personal Notes and Reflections

What mentioned in Chapter 2 that I can relate to?	Is there anything I have observed that I could add?	What in my view is the Christian diet of the day? What am I consuming?	Any other comments

CHAPTER 3

REROUTING

The Art and Science - Individual

The term 'cultured' is reserved for referring to someone who demonstrates refined taste, good manners and a rounded education, which includes the arts and literature – an erudite individual. It also speaks to one who exhibits a learned behaviour... a means of identification. In Biology, however, it is the process of incubating viruses or bacteria from tissue or other body fluids for the purpose of ... identification.

The microorganism is allowed to grow under controlled laboratory conditions. The result of this process informs physicians how these organisms grow and what type of environment they need for multiplication to occur. It also apprises doctors of the inverse, which is equally pertinent, particularly as we seek treatment options for the ailments they inflict. Clinicians want to know what will inhibit their growth...what is their - kryptonite. What will stop them from multiplying?

For human beings or microbes to be cultured, both require an environment, and there is always an outward demonstration of the effects of the environment on the individual or pathogen. For the microbes, they replicate or multiply, remain dormant or – die. On the other hand, humans demonstrate some key attributes, including a preference for a certain type of music, amongst other artistic expressions. They are careful where and what they eat. There is a distinct dress style or fashion. To be referred to as cultured means they are an avid reader, which impacts and influences their vocabulary and language. This individual must exhibit good manners and be 'educated'. In other words, a label is weightless. All weight is attributed to the - actions - of the cultured individual.

From the above, we can conclude certain conditions are necessary for growth, behaviours, and expressions, and these conditions could be positive or negative and may lead to dormancy or even death. The inputs have their corresponding outputs. There is clear evidence of the impact of the input confirming that interactions with an environment will affect either party... albeit sometimes more so on one than the other. And this is the process by which one is cultured - whether in the home, work, or church. This interaction produces outward characteristics. It becomes how we are identified as individuals and as a collective.

At various stages of our lives, we may or may not set out to adopt aspects of a culture or to embed parts of our original culture, which may be diminishing. Whatever we decide, the action is governed by certain principles. As culture is not genetically passed down, it is learnt, removing one thing and replacing it with another or adding something to what already exists – it doesn't just happen, nor does a state of dormancy. Being dormant is because of an intention or a made-up mind – not to adopt. So, you wait – wait it out.

Wait for the right environment. Changing culture is akin to being de-schooled and retaught. It takes approximately ten weeks to form a habit and between thirty and sixty days for it to break. Imagine being comfortable and secure in certain habits your entire life ... a decade or a year even. Habit forming or breaking is no easy feat. It is known to demand a mammoth portion of one's strength and will to break old practices and possibly an even greater chunk of motivation to fully embrace new behaviours. Like an addict on a course to break old cravings, it demands a mental and sometimes a physical cleansing as well.

That cleansing is what we usually refer to as a – detox. Detoxification is the process by which the blood is cleansed. In years past, it was a medical procedure where the individual had to depend on or wait for the medical team to decide to administer. This is akin to waiting for the pastor, the pastoral team, or the church to lead the way or to mandate the changes. Changes that, on your own, you feel incapable of initiating.

However, it has since been co-opted into the health-conscious craze and involves all manner of do-it-yourself processes. This cleansing can be done via several pathways. Take the bloodstream, for instance - impurities are removed from the liver, which is the body's principal filter responsible for processing and eliminating toxic substances. Or the kidneys, whose participation promotes fluid and electrolyte balance.

The immune system is another route, and that includes the lymphatic system. Not to be ignored is the body's largest organ

– the skin, which also plays a role during a body detox. Then, there is the respiratory tract, allowing for gaseous exchange and pH balance. As it pertains to the humble feet – not to be left out, adhesive pads are applied during sleep when toxins are drawn out of the body through the soles.

In the case of an addiction – a detox is the process by which the colon is cleansed of the addictive substance such as alcohol and other drugs. All traces are removed in preparation for a physically and mentally stable person who is ready to start therapy aimed at overcoming that - addiction.

People have various views about detox. They also have various ways of administering one, as outlined above. However, the church community should be united in spirit and vision. It should be able to recognise when a detox is necessary. It should have one belief, and that is - to put away all that is evil and hold fast to what is good. Likewise, there is only one way of administering the detox, and that is by drawing near to God. James 4:7-10 tells us to resist the contaminator, the devil, and he will flee from us.

It continues – draw near to God, and He will draw near to you – then cleanse your hands, you sinners, purify your hearts, and double-minded. As we draw near to God, He convicts us of sin, and we, in turn, seek cleansing at the cross. Through prayer, fasting, and the Word, we are cleansed, and by fellowshipping with brethren in Christ, we are built-up – and this is the prescribed package. It is not either or - but all the above.

Studies have shown that usually, people want to undergo a detox or want to change but - are either afraid of the process and corresponding risks or the financial burden it may carry. But yes, they want to eliminate the many symptoms it is said to eliminate. From bloating and joint pains to headaches and depression – to name a few. Who wouldn't want a flatter abdomen and glowing skin, for example?

However, achieving this is highly unlikely outside of the possible risks and discomfort the process demands.

It will cost something.

While it is one thing to consider taking action, a totally different mindset is required to do so. It is usual that following a process of information gathering and review, an informed decision is made. In this case, to undergo the detox process or not to detox. Each person must arrive at that decision for themselves. In the same way, the leaders of the organisation must examine honestly their appetite for change. Even when the evidence is overwhelming in favour of an alteration in our behaviour, we still find it incredibly challenging to change - and several responders confessed to finding it difficult to arrive at a decision.

There may be many people advising you or whispering in the undergrowth something about your post-lockdown weight gain; you may or may not think you have - or even consider it something of significance ... but do they really matter? Even when you go shopping, and like me, you realise you are not a perfect size 12 anymore. This means that before Lockdown, I didn't have to don a piece of clothing before leaving the store. Irrespective of which retail shop I would have left with a high degree of certainty, it would fit. Not so now. My excuse is that some shops have become less generous with the material, which may be your excuse too.

And we make all sorts of excuses and rationales packaged in well-rehearsed lines ready to be presented as to why we think we haven't really gained much weight, if any at all. In other words, it's a shop thing - manufacturer's fault... nothing to do with me. Until, one day at work or at home or out shopping for another dress – when you don't feel as agile as you once did. Neither mentally nor physically. You rationalised that, although you can't seem to shake the discomfort or the recognition that – you are just not managing. Your mood is not the same. It is difficult to see the day through. Your social circle diminishes, and your livelihood is threatened. You – take the decision to seek help. In the case of an addict, it is said the first sign of help is when that individual admits being in a place where they feel powerless and that their life has become unmanageable.

Several years ago, I was privileged to be a part of the Mentor Leadership Programme (MLP), a course initiated by my local church. Along with three other students, we were tasked with visiting a well-known 'mega-church' (not mega by American standards, but considerably large nonetheless). We were to observe 'how things are done around here'. Any 'indirect' shared leaning. Not with the expectation that one visit would yield all the answers, and it didn't; however, we could see from the way our party of four was greeted with bright smiles by uniformed ushers in a tastefully decorated foyer, complete with a dispenser serving a wide variety of both hot and cold drinks as well as some light snacks - at a cost, that we were in for an experience.

We all commented on how quickly we were spotted in what we thought was an incredibly busy thoroughfare. We were escorted in like visiting dignitaries to the next available seats while the 7 members of the worship team sang lustrously – shortly after which the service, unmoderated, got underway. Each presenter stepped confidently to the podium in a queue, and from the programme, neither went over their allotted time.

At the time for worship in giving, we could not miss the beautifully decorated envelopes - "Sow into the Harvest", resting in the rear pocket of the padded chair in front. It had the QR code and bank details imprinted, while ahead, displayed in large print across the cinema-like screen, were similar instructions on how to give along with the bank details. There were multiple card readers and containers being passed from end to end. The mood was jolly. Everyone seemed happy.

We were all surprised when, in such a large gathering of what looked like over a thousand people, everyone knew just when to say "amen" or "in Jesus' name" and when it was time for the reading of the scripture, prayer or the address from the host pastor, everyone stood without being told. All visitors were welcomed during the service, and first-time visitors were invited to stand, followed by a handshake from the person closest to them. On the way out of the vast sanctuary, no one recognised us or attempted to give us a special greeting.

No pastor was waiting at any of what I thought was about 6 large double doors to shake hands, imploring us enthusiastically to visit again, and the uniformed ushers had disappeared; in their place were instructors pointing the way out. Of course, we could not resist the temptation to check out the ladies' room. It was nothing short of a star-rated experience. It was well-lit with a pair of matching medium size chandeliers and white and dark marble tops.

Huge bouquets of fresh flowers marked the end of each counter adjacent floor to ceiling mirrors as well as wide horizontal wall mounted mirrors on top of each counter. There were scented candles scattered intentionally around – the perfect place to powder one's nose or smooth any travel crease. It was indeed an experience over there in London.

Each welcome bag had several similar items: tissue, a few mints, and after a thorough rummage through, quickly the name and email address were easy to see - should anyone decide to join a particular group or in need of any further information. Upon leaving, we collected the ticket, which allowed us to exit the free - car park – and before long, we joined the queue filing out, as we compared the constraints of our local church with the luxury being enjoyed by another.

It is said, a good culture is formed best in an environment where the right attitude and behaviours are highlighted and affirmed. Less time seeking to invalidate what is wrong and more focus on celebrating what is right. By adopting this approach, many will notice and catch on to what is expected in the spirit of the adage ... action speaks louder than words. It is uncertain what their route to where they had arrived was.

Truth be told, that one visit made us curious as to what another visit would be like but more so what other services, such as Bible study and prayer meetings and even more importantly and for the most part of the drive home, we mulled over the possible ills of the smaller groups: would we feel just as welcome, would we be given opportunities by the leader, would we be mentored and encouraged to exercise our spiritual gifts ...? Although the benefits of small groups are inconclusive, they continue to be part of the model used by churches to engage with their members, particularly as they increase in size.

Difficult to know the answer to those and the many other questions we had, as the geographical manoeuvres did not permit a subsequent visit. And one would be tempted to think that is the epitome of success and that there goes the result of a place with the 'right culture'. It would be interesting to see what, if any, their post-pandemic environment looks like. What changes, if any, have they had to make. What is included in their reset strategy... or if they need one.

During the year-long conversation and gathering of information, while poor bathroom facilities were mentioned, I cannot recall anyone complaining about the size of their church, the absence of chandeliers or even the monotony of the monochrome offering envelopes. Not to say those accessories would be unwelcome.

The absence of an understanding of one's individual 'calling' and own church building just about made it into the conversations, and the sometimes-poor sound quality, as well as the inconvenience of not having access to a card reader or where to park on a Sunday - but not so much the absence of a snack dispenser or the very friendly ushers ready to meet and greet. Instead, echoes of poor interpersonal relationships, the absence of compassion and empathy, territorial behaviour and partiality and ... no meaningful teaching of the word – loom.

So, if Lock-down was the detox process, and as we seek to reconnect and understand the changing face of the community we serve, it would help to ascertain what is fuelling the new diet. What are people looking for or using to keep that perfect skin, flat abdomen or peace they sought?

Just to be clear – I am not an advocate for the socially accepted physical detox. And while church scanning for shared learning can be a means to an end in a culture of continuous improvement, church hopping is not beneficial. Absolutely not.

Change is not usually easy, but change is always occurring. Leaving the known for the unknown can be anxiety producing. Many have confessed to their decision to move on, not being an easy or impulsive one. Some still feel somewhat guilty about leaving and wonder why - why was it so difficult to walk away in search of a healthy church community that meets their needs.

In the analogy of the detox with aspects of some gruelling steps, many may recognise times when situations move an individual to arrive at a decision, which includes participation in the most unpleasant change process for the transformation to be realised. The eventual movement of people who have been through that mental process should serve as an acknowledgement that something must have impelled persons who were so addicted to their zone of comfortable discomfort – to choose to worship elsewhere, or not congregate at all - despite myriad programmes and different teams so innovatively conjured.

It is true that while the church is there to create the environment that facilitates spiritual growth, it is not the only tool, place of nurturing or the one space where maturity is facilitated. It is difficult to visit or spend an hour or three per week in a local church service and expect to grow or have it meet all the individual's needs. The limited time doesn't provide for adequate reflection on scripture for meaning in life, therefore the onus is also on the individual to be intentional, proactive, and fiercely committed to spiritual growth – by prioritising your relationship with God daily and with the support of the whole church community.

Personal Notes and Reflections

What is mentioned in Chapter 3 that I can relate to?	Anything I need to take a decision on?	What are my views on what is described	Any other comments

CHAPTER 4

REROUTING

Possible Route to the Ideal – Organisational

While the census highlights changes, it doesn't explain why things have changed. Feedback from the yearlong conversations as well as wider research, do not indicate a one-size-fits-all approach, recognising each context is different and each person's needs vary. We are all interacting with the rapidly changing external environment – and are impacted in different ways. This is a strong indicator that achieving the desired outcome demands a multifaced approach, both on an individual and a wider organisational level.

There has been an increase in online churches and a marked increase in YouTube channels. Several churches that were unknown, meaning in social media wilderness, have since announced themselves on social media platforms to varying degrees. Pastors who once scolded congregants for having a social media presence have now gone on to develop their personal sites and continue to engage in this way. Others have rebranded, employing anything suspected capable of delivering the desired outcome. While social media and branding, among other interventions, are important, beware, they serve only as an invite to the dinner party. Neither of them is the meal, nor do they serve as a guarantee for the quality of the company that is so necessary when at the dining table. And so, unfortunately, the social media drive on its own may not have changed much, if at all.

However, one would advise that the invitation continues to be sent. Continue to alert the community to what's on offer. Let them know what to expect from both the 'staff' and the product. As a church, we have a product – that is unquestionable. The question is, are we consistent in messaging and delivery? Do we have family members who understand the values and live out the culture? Are we prepared to be held accountable both by the guests and – our Lord and Saviour, Jesus Christ.

As there are many questions, many suggestions have been put forward as possible remedies for this illness. From more energised worship services to shorter sermons or increased community outreach programmes to present a more holistic approach to delivering the Good News. Many churches have had to do the inverse and have therefore altered how they engage with their local community as a reduction in resources limits capabilities and focus. Whatever is considered is usually done with good intentions – whether they are effective or not requires proper forecasting and planning and review of feedback.

The first item on the menu, recognise that while the dinner party guests may be from the same place, they have a change in requirement, or their request is more forceful. And the church is no different from secular organisations. Many people have resigned and either opted for early retirement or moved on to other places and types of ministries since the pandemic. Which could address the change in demographics only but doesn't answer all else.

One thing we can all agree on is that the evidence is clear and that something has changed or that an ongoing process of change is occurring. It is well known in the improvement space that a symptom is evidence of a deeper issue. It is unwise to try to fix what you think is the problem as opposed to what ...is – the issue(s) and to unearth that the '5-Whys approach' is usually employed. Toyota Industries founder Mr Sakichi developed this technique during the evolution of its manufacturing in the 1930s, and today, it is a critical component of the approach to problem solving.

It is believed that by asking 'Why?' 5 times, where each answer forms the basis of the next question, you can get to the root of the problem - Root Cause Analysis (RCA), and from an identification of the causal factors one can implement countermeasures. It is important that the answer to each 'why?' is grounded in fact. Don't be afraid to ask why, even after the 5th.

Likewise, be courageous to stop if the root cause is found after the 3rd, for example. Note that not all problems have a single root cause. Therefore, while the above technique can lead you to follow a single route, it may also flag the need to explore other options., Each of these techniques will need to be applied until you reach the root cause for each one.

The Problem: church membership is down, but attendance is up

(cited on scaredstructures.org, 2018)

1. **Why?** – People today resist joining the church. (First Why?)

2. **Why?** - They don't see a reason to commit (Second Why?)

3. **Why?** – They don't understand the benefits of the biblical reasons and expectations for membership in the Body of Christ. (Third Why?)

4. **Why?** – Because no one has taught them. (Fourth Why?)

5. **Why?** – Because the staff have not developed or prioritised the means to do that (Fifth Why? And root cause).

A real root cause should point to a process or behaviour that doesn't exist or has failed to work consistently.

In this case, staff development is indicated along with prioritisation of necessary resources for teaching and learning – a culture of improvement would help.

No one should be under any illusion that the '5 whys?', or any specific approach, can unearth all underlying causes. Quite likely, they will not flag that the root cause of an individual's behaviour is an incestuous or abusive environment, for example. Some of these issues require the gift of discernment or the presence of a perceived psychologically safe space – an open, empathetic, no-judgment culture.

In fact, Ernest and Young released their 2021 empathy in a business survey, which tracked how empathy affects leaders, employees, and innovation in the workplace. The survey of more than one thousand workers reveals that 88% felt that empathetic leadership creates loyalty in the face of great resignation. Many times, leaders are so busy ensuring the media equipment and other resources enabling a strong social media presence are perfect, or that the colour of the paint on the walls is just right, or that the ... but how do we conduct business within the aesthetically pleasing nicely scented four walls is of greater importance – and a word to describe that is culture.

Even more reason for us to be mindful of our biases, which feed the way we choose to interact with each other; not everything will be told, not everything will be discerned by everyone, but quite likely, everything will be – perceived. Many people who are no longer seen in our pews have moved on without giving an explanation, and while knowing the reasons behind their absence is useful for targeted interventions, there is also no obligation on their part to offer one.

Cultures evolve over time—sometimes slipping backwards, other times progressing with little challenge. Research has found that almost every enterprise that has attained peak performance—including Google, Apple, and Microsoft - got there by applying sound principles. They see culture through the lens of competitive advantage and an accelerator of change. The church can see culture through the lens of opportunity ..., the opportunity to invigorate, inspire, motivate, and energise congregants to grasp the bigger picture and to live out their faith in this present world, thus markedly affecting the external environment. The church needs to see itself as a unique channel of cultural influence.

And everyone will have their view about what the ideal culture needs to be for them. The high possibility of this difference of opinion leads researchers to warn of an acknowledgement of cultural intransigence. Therefore, begin to see culture as an enabler of shared understanding, connectedness and belonging, growth ...and not an impediment. It has the potential to move people and teams from apathy to achieve peak performance - peak performance as defined by agreed internal aims and goals.

Many books will advocate for a clear strategic plan, and strategy is necessary too; however, it is unwise of anyone to focus primarily on team strategy for achieving the desired outcome in place of its culture. Nothing gets done unless people move. Moving people move strategy. Moving people requires culture as the food to feed the actions. There should be synergy between both.

A popular word used by many churches to imply a homely, welcoming, inclusive environment is - family. However, within any family, work needs to be done, goals need to be achieved, and inadvertently or deliberately, some will seek to participate in the goal realisation process, while others may feel disconnected – even in said family.

Not only does everyone want to feel welcome, but they also want to feel seen and valued. The right culture can foster the above and create that all-important sense of connectedness. And a true teamwork ethos can be useful in achieving this. Unfortunately, teamwork can sometimes – inadvertently be relinquished to a buzzword only and do not reflect the word's true meaning. Where people are only invited to deliver the end product but omitted from the decision-making process.

However, it serves well to see it as a key cultural attribute to promote. After all, from evangelism to planning for other events and productions - all require a 'team' of people for them to be realised, and this must be a central feature in our churches. Not only is it a route for getting things done – but it is a way of mentoring and growing oneself and others, including future leaders. It enables kinship - another route to building long-term relationships and a way of realising the different skill sets that can add value.

And by recognising value in an individual does not mean the sole purpose of the individual is what they bring to the table – that can be easily recognised. And although people are dispensable, one should not be made - to feel- dispensable. A healthy balance is necessary for strengthening this sense of - or perceived connectedness.

By working in teams, one can quickly realise where their gifting lies... or does not. Who works best with whom because of their differences or similarities, strengths and opportunities for development can be observed. A team approach more than likely leaves no one behind; everyone has a sense of 'making a meaningful contribution'. The latter is key, particularly at a time when wide-scale meaningful change is to be made. Having a team culture can help reduce fear as members support each other. More importantly, in moments of a difference of opinion, they not only lead to patience and tolerance as we bear with and learn from each other but also add to the richness of output.

Review your place of worship periodically – from the congregation to the general community and contrast those nebulous hopes with what is specific to your place. What will add value? What is valued here? And it is one thing to have amazing ideas. However, the research tells us – the key lies in how things get done around here. There will always be some things that are found everywhere, such as a clean environment with comfortable chairs and vibrant activities for the elderly within the community – but there is something that is specific to an organisation – and that is - its culture.

If not yet done so – take the time to observe the behaviour prevalent in your place of worship.

Question, are we at our best?

Are we living our values – what are our values?

Is this the culture we want to flourish here?

If it isn't, then the old practices need to go, but which ones?

Which would you like to stop doing, and what would you replace it with?

Together, you must decide what your aspirations are.

As a church – how do we want new people to be treated?

How will team or departmental and whole church members' meetings be managed and structured?

How will feedback be dealt with – or invited?

How will difficult questions be received and addressed?

Do you know what positive or negative behaviours will most likely affect the current culture?

Could a focus group be pulled in to help answer this question?

How do you think members will react when the changes are implemented?

Who among you are respected leaders and are good at influencing the people they lead?

Who would be leading the training – for example, the new way for the usher team to meet and greet attendees – would an external voice add validity – or will an internal resource highlight people's value?

Watch out for our happier members with positive feedback – as a sign of it working as planned.

Be careful not to overwhelm yourself and your teams with big steps in one go; this can be counterproductive. Remember, a 'family' unit under strain would hardly likely want to think or look outside of itself. If those internal needs are unmet, it is very difficult to think of others.

Be prepared to be in this for the long haul – aim to embed. Create widely recognisable steps – mirrored by the leadership team and spoken of often. Hear from congregation members how they can reinforce the new practice in their smaller groups, departments and among themselves.

Celebrate each other.

Celebrate wins.

Celebrating each other makes people feel appreciated, and celebrating wins on a wider level – can motivate people to take the next step.

Encourage candour- the quality of being open and honest – respectful frankness. The practice will soon begin to spread organically - peer-to-peer.

Mentioned in a previous chapter is the other side of an affiliation with the past, which has immobilised some organisations. It's tempting to dwell on the negative traits of existing culture. However, it is important to note that corporate culture is usually born out of the best intentions and the context and values that existed at that time. All of these have worked together and brought you to where you are, and you will have many sound attributes.

It is, therefore important to look for the strengths in your existing culture. For example, they might include a deep commitment to evangelism and outreach but have evolved over time into a predisposition towards being outward-focused at the expense of strengthening internal relationships and regard for integrity.

Seek ways to demonstrate the relevance of the original values. This can be done by revisiting stories highlighting the good they have brought and why people can still believe in them. Recognise that bringing what is known to the forefront can serve to lessen the anxieties of the unknown and increase scale and pace because it will be received as a shared development. While doing so, look out for the people who really want to help – hone this strength and use it when interacting with members.

Empower other members to voice what this means for them and have these supporters or champions share how it can be lived out. If they look hard enough, most churches will find they already have many people who practice the desired behaviours. As a church family, try to incorporate the informal, more softer side of the body. Review and, if necessary, adjust reporting lines or chain of command, decision rights, delivery model and processes.

Encourage frequent fellowship and networking interest groups. Quick to engage in ad hoc conversations. Remember, fellowship meetings won't necessarily lead to closer relationships unless they are structured intentionally for closer connections to form. Seek to reach congregants at an emotional level – invoke that sense of pride and altruism through social visits, ad hoc meetings, and impromptu midweek telephone discussions.

Be interested – not to know someone's business but to see where you could point them for help with that health condition, a truant child - a burdensome teacher or an oppressive workplace culture. Be interested in what is a source of distraction or deep concern for our fellow church brothers and sisters. Intercession is a good place to start.

Ask the all-knowing – all-seeing God- to reveal the issues and what support is needed, then follow through beyond saying – 'I am praying for you' – to, if possible, offer practical support as well.

Speak to a wide cross-section of members and visitors too. Reflect on how people are feeling. Demonstrate that you are listening. Let them know they are heard and their concerns are taken seriously. That they matter. Create rapport with new members early on to create that sense of community and belonging. Measuring and monitoring cultural progress at each stage is essential to prevent 'backsliding', correct course where needed, and demonstrate tangible evidence of improvement.

One such improvement could come from feedback or a notable decrease in the number of complaints.

Review departmental leads living up to their commitments to key actions aimed at embedding the new practice. This could include looking at basics such as arriving on time - and managing departmental or members' meetings to end on stated time, demonstrating that people's time is respected. When designing cultural metrics, remember that you get what you measure.

So, an overemphasis on quarterly attendance results, for example, can create an impersonal culture – of seeking 'bums on seats.' This can trigger inappropriate pressure on valued relationships and negatively impact growth. Remember, numbers on their own can be erroneous. It would help to review the number of 'repeat' visitors and/or conversion to membership.

If, as a church, building relationships is the primary focus, then measuring the number of "engagements with members and general visitors more often" can be a critical review point. It could be measured as the number of calls or check-ins per week. However, ensure calls are meaningful and not relegated to a tick box exercise.

Similarly, focusing on retention metrics as an indication of overall engagement and role or 'ministry' satisfaction may not be as useful—or as important—as what happens to the retention of 'top performers' once a cultural initiative gets underway. No need for extensive, cumbersome new measurement systems – weekly feedback from attendees via a simple 3 to maximum 5-point survey will do. The result could also serve as a way of enforcement. Observe the behaviours of those who have a high impact on the experiences of others, such as those in leadership positions and are widely respected.

The pastor/leader also needs to be detoxed from his or her sentimental attachment. Be aware of your own biases formed out of personal values – and look to see if these values are congruent with the wider church values – because if no one else buys into what's been sold - it should be the pastor and leadership teams. Note also - a top-down approach will slow the implementation process. However, the pastor and leadership all need to lead by example.

Nothing creates disconnect quicker or more broadly than poor or lack of communication. A well-developed communication plan or engagement strategy is helpful. Most secular teams have weekly or monthly meetings, which are upscaled according to project demand. Communication in many forms is necessary to eliminate exclusion as people receive and interpret information differently, particularly persons with hidden disabilities.

Church members' meetings are as important as gatherings for other meetings. Solidifying buy-in, creating inclusion, and reducing the knowledge power gap is key to any team or organisation. Those who know can appear superior to those who don't know. And while basking in ignorance is ill-advised, leaders have a duty to ensure all pertinent information is disseminated.

This is critical if the two-tier entitled - in-crowd- culture is to be eliminated from the church. Of course, there is something for the Board, or as a matter of confidentiality, it is divulged on a need-to-know basis. No one should know until all, or the majority present, are told that it is for a few – particularly believers who are en route to a certain maturity level. Many people use information as a way of wielding power, and an uncomfortable truth is that this occurs at various levels of the church.

Members' meetings should be a place where ideas are shared. With heads together – diverse ideas are actively sought and generated, as everyone comes with different experiences and backgrounds. It should not be the leaders' telling others what is happening – but a two-way process facilitated. Discussions are had about the overall life and mission of the church.

It is an important aspect of the governance of the church.

These wider meetings are important for collaboration and accountability. Regular meetings should help eliminate the build-up of issues to discuss and reduce conflict. It is imperative that God is glorified even during the business meeting. That humility is exercised is paramount with prayer and entertaining the Holy Spirit's presence as decisions are made.

Usually, where a poor culture exists, members' meetings are absent. This could reflect fear of conflict and poor relationships, where fear of confrontation renders others voiceless to give peace of mind to the leader and possibly a few. It could also be a way of intimidation born out of lack of confidence, or it could be a system of control and bullying - indicating it is one person or a group of persons' way or the 'highway'. All of these indicate a need for training, mentorship, and where outlined, agreed behavioural expectations and conduct could help... and with consistency over time – a routine or habit is formed, resulting in a meeting culture.

It is necessary that these meetings reflect the corporate culture. Therefore, the chairperson and membership should exercise the fruit of the spirit, grace and ... timekeeping, which is sometimes taken for granted but can be a reason for disgruntlement or absenteeism. Encourage transparency – make it a place where ill-conceived narratives can be addressed and, if necessary, where the whole church can participate in a meaningful discourse around cultural redress.

While en route to the ideal, try to draw on the positive aspects of your culture where possible. Turn them to your advantage and offset some of the negative aspects as you go. This approach makes change far easier to implement. The leaders have the task of motivating, influencing and inspiring people to become. Start with that passion and belief that as you learn and grow together, everyone will benefit as you get deeper and wider – bigger in your knowledge of the truth and rise up to God's Highways. Practising like Daniel – to a high standard with that spirit of excellence. Seek to reinforce any longtime strengths that have eroded over time.

When people feel heard and appreciated, escalate the plan for change. That sense of pride reinvigorates and rebuilds enthusiasm and a genuine love for each other. Bear in mind what is within our gift as we acknowledge that many things are outside our control. For example, people will leave no matter what we do. However, with the right environment, people are more likely to remain. We live in a fast-moving world – and an equally dynamic church environment. The term 'microwave' society has been used to describe a 'get it now', 'do it now', or 'I want it now' mindset.

And while make hay while the sun shines, why leave for tomorrow what can be done today, or take the opportunity while you can? These are all useful advice, but acknowledge that they may play out very differently in context.

However, the description should alert the church family that context does not negate the possibility of new family members being unable to exercise patience. This means the 'now' culture may impact the expectations of newcomers who may leave before forming a connection as the church family – eventually gets around to exhibiting what is expected. Which is that, among other things, we are indeed kind, loving and compassionate. And that Kingdom values and culture will be made obvious ...at some point.

If not now, then ... when?

Can we afford to not live daily according to the dictates of our culture?

Mathew 5:14-16 tells us – "You are the light of the world. A city that is set on a hill cannot be hidden. Nor do they light a lamp and put it under a basket, but on a lampstand, and it gives light to all who are in the house. Let your light so shine before men, that they may see your good works and glorify your Father in heaven."

To recapitulate, culture changes over time. Environmental scanning should be an ongoing process. Some suggested leadership checks include:

Is this healthy? If so – what makes it a place for growth – who decided that this is 'healthy' or how it should be?

How has the congregation changed over time - how is this reflected in the leadership team?

Do leaders recognise they are not always right and that they won't always have all the answers?

Culture change, like many other change initiatives, comes with a price. The price to pay may include resignations - as the people who are no longer served by the new culture may leave. Leaders must be prepared to have those uncomfortable conversations or to face the unintentional 'falling away that may occur?

Like any organisation, think of the lifecycle of the church. For secular organisations, Alfred Marshall's theory of the 1890s states that, similar to living organisms, organisations experience 5 stages of change as they grow and mature: birth to growth, maturity to decline – renewal. A mature organisation, he states, is in danger of stagnation and failure to innovate, while at the decline stage, it becomes a self-perpetuating bureaucracy with slowed growth and diminished returns. But at renewal, this phase can take many forms; a change or reorganisation in the right direction can restore its health.

Tony Morgan, the Founder and Lead Strategist for the Unstuck Group (2023), states that most churches start, grow, thrive, decline and eventually – end. But the Lord of the harvest – Jehovah God's intention is that they grow to maturity and maintain a state of sustained health even during periods of change in traditions, methods, and cultural practices. Remember, what got you here won't necessarily be the route to where you intend to go – the qualities that brought a church to its current level of ministry and fruitfulness will likely not propel it to the next level.

It helps if leaders seek to start with what's strong, not what's wrong. See what's already out there. Talk to people. Involve people first and foremost...talk to the Lord of the harvest (Luke 10:22).

Personal Notes and Reflections

What mentioned in Chapter 4 that I can relate to?	Is there anything I have observed that I could add?	What is my view on the way back – or forward?	Any other comments

CHAPTER 5

Embed

Scale and scope – Business as Usual.

According to anthropologists, culture is a broad term that refers to social norms and behaviours that are prevalent in three layers: international, national, and local subcultures. These subcultures could be – government, corporate or religious. Another popular definition of culture is that put forward by Swiss American psychologist, Edgar Schein, who states that culture is:

"A pattern of shared basic assumptions learned by a group as it solved its problems of external adaptation and internal integration, which has worked well enough to be considered valid and, therefore, to be taught to new members as the correct way to perceive, think, and feel in relation to those problems."

Assumptions are the underlying beliefs held by each member within the local church and are said to be significant indicators of the 'true' culture. It is how members work together. Behaviours and ways of communicating. How success and failure are dealt with. What people really think of each other and the leadership. These assumptions are shaped by what is taught, seen, and vocalised at all levels of the organisation.

By Schein's definition, these assumptions are formed overtime... which indicate, for culture change – leaders must be committed to a process – be in it for the long haul. However, there are several factors that can enhance or vitiate the quality of the shared assumptions and impact the scale and scope at which the culture is socialised and adapted within a church environment.

Highlighted below are some foundational imperatives to consider:

1. Repentance, fasting and prayer

2. Teach all of scripture

3. Beware of pride

4. Encourage Humility

Repentance, Fasting and Prayer.

Maybe many of you can testify to the validity of either the '5 Whys?' approach or any of the other suggestions made above... having employed it or all of them yourself. If that is so, that is great. I hope there is an even greater number of you who have employed - and with much more frequency, the principle of continuous repentance, frequent fasting and fervent in prayer approach. Together they are central to the testimony of the cultured remnants, who speak of their ability to reveal not only what, but ... who, why, where - how and when.

They are known to transform the person who participates wholeheartedly and honestly in the process as time is spent apart with God intentionally and meaningfully. The one who is unconcerned about 'saving face' and truly intent on turning away from sinful acts to being transformed. Both gospels, Mark 1.35 and St. Luke 5.16 highlight a very important practice which Jesus himself regularly engaged in as He withdrew to spend time alone with God.

That individual relationship is critical if our life is to bear fruit the father expects. It has profound benefits: It provides the optimal environment to be deeply rooted in Christ and to realise sustained peace, joy, and an overflow of hope. This hope gives joy and changes our disposition. Through this medium we are reminded to seek the continual grace and renewal of the Holy Spirit in our lives and that is important if we are to listen critically to ourselves, the world in which we live and carefully to one another. True repentance is rooted in humility – it is humbling.

Romans 3:22 tells us that we are made right with God through faith in Him – says: even the righteousness of God, through faith in Jesus Christ, to all [a]and on all who believe. For there is no difference; for all have sinned and fall short of the glory of God, being justified freely by His grace through the redemption that is in Christ Jesus. The act of repentance should be a continual event.

For the cultured individual, repentance is a lifestyle. They know it evokes gratitude and sensitivity to hearing God - leading to obedience. And it is from this place of gratitude to God that we extend grace to each other. Many times, we only have room to see faults in ourselves or through the lens of envy and self-debasement - but genuine repentance changes the mind and thought patterns - and ultimately the way you think about yourself, and the way you view others. It is through repentance that habits and patterns are broken, and room is made in the heart for the Word of God to exercise its power to change the individual.

Their transformative effects cannot be hidden.

It is not enough for repentance prayer and fasting to be part - of our culture, but that they should be woven into the very fabric of our cultural identity and an integral staple of our diet is imperative. Through fasting that focus is taken away from self and situations to be placed on God. As the broader culture adopts more of the secular, increasingly, human beings rely on themselves and what is created as opposed to turning to be totally dependent on God the creator.

Fasting is another way to humble oneself. It counters the pride of self-reliance as the individual seeks a Godly lifestyle. The cultured person lives a life which includes not only continual repentance but frequent fasting. In the cultured remnants, one can hear and see the effects of those fasting and prayer sessions that are not necessarily mandated by the pastor. Those personal fasting sessions that no one knows is taking place in the privacy of the home of individuals or their inner closet.

The one where you emerge a stone lighter in worldly pounds, fresh from physical detox, but many stones heavier under the anointing of the Holy Spirit - after being filled from being laid out on The Therapist's couch ... listening, feasting, and growing. Freed of your additions and worldly culture with its accompanying negative ways of thinking and being - relinquished.

It's telling. You begin to be - 'telling'.

And by telling, I mean showing. You then bring forth the fruit. Not the waving of one's pinkie with the hope that it will indicate we are cultured - doesn't that a cultured Christian make. Christlike actions, behaviours and mannerisms carry the most weight. The actions, such as self-discipline and self-control. There is a sense of accountability. That fruit looks something like – no longer can the dining experience incorporate food from the world's table.

You are careful in your conversations and selective with what you hear and your source of information. You carry the knowledge that cultured people are refined in their behaviour and mannerisms, so it is no longer palatable to engage with or participate in activities that lead to the wounding or debasement of each other. You are careful to guard your character – your integrity matters. Giving glory to God matters – that He gets the glory in all that you do is integral to your new way of being.

Your music is like King David's, borne out of that one-to-one lived experience with God and your relationship with your wide social circle, which is primarily comprised of members of the family of believers. You seek to be sound in doctrine – not moved by soundbites and echoes placed on repeats, as it is with those busy getting on with whatever aspects of life appeal to their outer conjured peace – a peace defined in conjunction with societies' determinants. Instead, you possess the peace which surpasses human understanding.

You appear .... cultured.

The cultured person not only lives a life of continual repentance, is frequently fasting, and is also fervent in prayer. During prayer, all cares are cast on Jesus, who replaces all heaviness with a garment of praise. Gratitude and authority have replaced doubt and fear. The way you interpret and make sense of the world is through the lens of faith in the sovereign Lord's will being done here on earth as it is in heaven – and you desire His will being done in your life and that it extends to others too.

There is humility in your disposition and justice on your tongue, with serving, volunteering, or ministering at the forefront of your mind. Others notice and comment. Some favourable, others not so much but you hold fast – intentional, knowing it starts with you. And that is something we should all accept – change begins with us.

The reasons behind the erosion of our culture that created the 'context', can be addressed because it is rooted in sin. Accepting that is akin to accepting that the poor will always be with us, as Jesus said in Mark 14:7, meaning some things will never exist. And as there are levels of poverty, so too are different ways that each context presents - therefore, the 'context' will always exist to varying degrees. We know this because we live in an unregenerated world - where the effects of the fall will continue to be seen and felt until this old earth makes way for the new heaven and the new earth (Revelation 21).

The further away we are from God, the poorer we are in spirit ...and morals, and the more consumed we are with pride and other sinful practices. The closer we are to God, the more open we are to seeing the needs of others and being responsive even to the one who is both resourceful and spiritually poor. And while we occupy this earth until He returns, or should we be called home before His second coming, we have a duty of care for each other. Not to cast off or condemn, but to do what Mark 12:30-31 reminds us, which is to love others as we do ourselves. This is how the world will identify us.

This is what they expect to see when they walk into our midst, whether in a church building or place of work – or wherever we may be at any given time – the cultured person cares about the spiritual and social welfare of others and actively intercedes on their behalf.

Bear in mind the world may expect to see tired-looking chairs occupying our church buildings, or they may expect a sermon on a Sunday morning. They may even expect an outdoor summer activity, but I believe there are still many who will not be expecting an uncultured Kingdom family. This is where many become disillusioned. We say the church is made up of people – and although some use hypocrites to describe people of faith – there are still many who come into our church community thinking this has got to be different from the workplace, where there may be dysfunctionality and racism.

Some pastors reported that COVID-19 fundamentally disrupted routine ways of doing ministry. Thanks to limited time in the sanctuary in the unsettling post-lockdown space, some have seized the opportunities presented and have bravely changed the way church is done in several ways. However, we still need to catch up in terms of - the way we are ... as a church.

So, it is not a quantitative approach to what is to be implemented but more of a qualitative one - seeking a psychologically safe environment conducive to all. Get back to recognising – embracing and living the fact that the church is God's governing body here on earth. Being intentional about how we disciple and catechise individuals.

To mitigate the risk of sending a message that one moment you bear no semblance of the kingdom culture and then suddenly you fully exhibit its characteristics, let me hasten to say that being cultured doesn't happen overnight – it occurs over time.

Intentionality is critical to our faith journey. Think ... detox.

Through the continuous practice of genuine repentance, fasting and prayer – being empowered by the Holy Spirit- the inner man is strengthened and able to take the steps needed for sustained reset. Over time, aspects of the individual's old cultural practices that are antagonistic to or do not align with being regenerated – born again or the new birth - are eliminated to make room for the new you that is ready to connect and is determined to grow.

Teach all of Scripture

Data suggests that churches will continue to struggle to thrive and are unlikely to halt a steep decline unless teachings such as that of the Patriarchs (Abraham, Isaac, and Jacob) are re-embraced and brought back to the fore. Their lives help us understand faith and the implications of total obedience to God, purpose and sovereignty corresponding with man's responsibility. And these can sometimes be difficult to grasp.

The King James Bible phrases and cadences influenced the spoken and written mode of communication of some of our nation's founding fathers, while its ideas shaped their habits and informed their political experiment. This proves that biblical teaching was part of different aspects of society and has left its mark - even on the political culture and not just the church community- over the years. We must know that gaining and retaining a sound knowledge of God – The Creator is worthwhile. The importance of sound biblical teaching cannot be overemphasised. The word of God is God's Word. It is what God wants us to know and has chosen to have them recorded for our benefit. The Word of God not only tells us the meaning of life but includes how to live in this world and, in particular, how to live, work - and do life with each other – which is key to culture formation and sustainability.

Another means by which culture is formed and embedded is by espoused values. Espoused values are what an organisation says about its culture and ways of doing things and are, therefore important to note.

Along with mission and value statements, they too are means of communicating cultural norms: the mission statement, list of values or even a periodic newsletter are good ways of providing insight - however, the aim should be for the set of shared assumptions to reflect the espoused values. People look for espoused values primarily in the organisation's goals and objectives, and when these are seen, there is increased faith in the company's ability to hold themselves accountable. And that is admittedly – not always easy.

One way of achieving this in our churches is by cultivating a 'sameness' in our belief system. And that should be rooted in scripture rightly divided. We must be clear about what we believe and why. Start with what is already known and build on the existing knowledge. Be consistent in messaging. Continuous teaching of the word of God is pivotal. Biblical teaching helps eliminate other cultural biases, such as those exhibited in evangelism.

This bias limits the scope of who we share the gospel with and who we see as reachable or less so. It could lead to racial or cultural diversity in our churches. Leaders can use sound doctrinal principles to eliminate or minimise its development. Biblical teachings speak to the work of the cross, which should help to nullify unhelpful perceptions of others and our interactions with people from different social cultures.

By understanding and practising biblical principles, we are more likely to be considerate. Therefore, we consider other factors affecting the lived experience of the people we engage with directly or those further afield. We look outside of ourselves and observe the effects of factors such as poverty, accessibility to resources in the community, or language ability, and seek a just and fair church community as well as an equitable society. There is a blessing for those who will keep and apply these principles. It brings healing to the body. The Word of God is life; its life-changing power should not be underestimated (Hebrews 4:12). The Word of God transforms our lives. The Word of God revolutionises families, whole communities, and, ultimately, the world. And that – Is. A. Fact.

Daily, we read and hear from mistruths and half-truths to blatant lies – by the way ... irrespective of the degree to which it veers from the truth, is inconsequential and not a point to debate. It should be seen in the context of truth or a lie. There is no grey area in scripture. To see grey is to open our minds or pierce our headpiece. Holes, irrespective of size, act as portals and eventually make room for the enemy - satan. It attempts to draw us into conversation with the spirits of the Pharisees and Sadducees and, ultimately, the evil one, whose aim is to deceive those who can be easily beguiled. And we are experiencing this at an alarmingly increasing rate. It pervades the air.

Sound Biblical teaching guards the individual against false teachings and helps to solidify one's Kingdom culture. It creates an environment for discerning what is from God and prepares the individual for passing on said principles to the next generation. We must be careful where and what we eat. In studying the Word of God - every word matters. Every part of speech matters. The tense and how the words occur matter. It is compared to a sword, a powerful instrument with discerning ability. It takes the individual to the very depths of their personality... helps them to see and know things about themselves they would not otherwise have uncovered. It is the most powerful instrument for combating the lies from satan, the deceiver. It is also noted to be a powerful weapon in anyone's or any leader's armour as they seek to address the characteristics of their local church. The Word of God analyses and gives access to the very nature of a thing.

It is the Word of God because it ... came from God. It is information He wants us to know. Information that penetrates what is of the soul and what is from the spirit. As human beings created in God's likeness and image, we reflect His triune nature. This means where He is Father, Son and Holy Spirit, we are body, soul and spirit, and it is only by the Word of God that we learn to distinguish between the spirit and the soul. Sadly, many of us have been sucked into these erroneous teachings and are growing more and more sympathetic to the humanist's way of life when it is from the Word of God that we get the answer to the meaning of life.

It is taught well in a cultured environment. Where there is a good culture – there are good, sound Bible study sessions. Both students and teachers are enthusiastic and visibly affected by the teaching. The Bible is recognised as relevant and current. It is regarded as the most influential book ever and esteemed highly with unapologetic reverence.

B.F. Skinner, an American psychologist, behaviourist, inventor, and social philosopher of the 1930s, said learning is progressive, requires an intentional attitude, and involves a shift in overt behaviour. It works well in a culture where a learning environment is facilitated. Similar to - for example, in our secular role, where we seek to learn and grow and hone our craft, so too should each person who has accepted Christ should the call to learn, grow and mature. Where there is continuous teaching of the Word of God, and learning is occurring – there is unmissable growth and maturity. Growth in faith in the Word.

Unfortunately, where there are uninspiring, lacklustre sessions, this can leave people deflated and ready to move on. A good culture aims to keep Bible study sessions inspiring and dynamic.... It helps people to welcome it not as the word of man or simply from the teacher or preacher but as the Word of God (1 Thessalonians 2:13), which effectively works in those who believe.

Attendees must be taught to receive the teaching with faith in its authenticity and the knowledge that the Bible reads the individual. Having said that, all is not lost – if you feel you don't already have faith – it is obtainable by hearing the Word of God (Romans 10:17).

Hearing as illustrated in Proverbs 4: Give full attention to His words, incline your ear to what He has to say...develop a need to learn. Do not let the Word depart from your eyes...see it for yourself (the eye gate to learning) – look at it repeatedly – focus. And keep The Word of God in your heart – the very place that springs forth the issues of life, meaning what is in your heart will determine the course of your life – guard your heart with the Word.

Over time, faith is born and grown. Faith is important for the Word to be effective in our lives. The Word of God must be received in faith. The Word of God must take first-place in the life of the believer and in the life of the congregation. It is the food that feeds the cultured diet.

From the Word of God, culture and cultured giants grow.

Pre-COVID, one of the main things to consider in our Bible study sessions was that many participants are not necessarily from churched homes, impacting delivery. However, post-COVID, there is another hurdle: increasingly, more sessions are taking place on a virtual platform. This poses many additional challenges, from Wi-Fi connectivity affecting any or all the attendees to imagination and creativity as a particular implication for the teacher.

Very easily, attendees, who at the end of another busy workday, finally find themselves in the comfort of their homes, can be easily present in the name on camera but could quite possibly be otherwise engaged or may well have fallen asleep. It is also helpful if all attendees are in a place where there are little to no distractions, which, being in a home environment, may not always be possible. It is not that the engagement or learning is solely the facilitator's responsibility; however, it is always helpful to have a properly planned teaching (not preaching) session executed with passion and anointing that considers the different learning styles of the attendees.

This could be an indication of appropriate training for those who are tasked with teaching the Word in our local churches. Sometimes, there is blatant disregard for the attendee's time as the session either starts late or is overrun. Teachers must be careful while seeking to be led by the Spirit – that is indeed the case- and not indulge in a topic that has nothing to do with the subject matter for which they have prepared or the participants have anticipated.

All the above and others you may identify can lead to non-attendance and ultimately lack of growth as there are people who - on their own, do not fully grasp the meaning of the text or may struggle with literacy or other hidden disabilities, and therefore turn to other 'teachers'. Share resources to assist with individual study. This is important to eliminate erroneous material that may inadvertently make its way into the hands of the unsuspecting, and the nature of the seed sown in us determines the nature of the fruit we bear.

It is said that where someone is being fed is where they will go – there is a psychological state of being fed in your own house. Also, of possibly even greater importance is the recognition that it is in reading and studying the Word of God that we are often most challenged and made to feel frustrated - sometimes overtaken by human-inspired answers.

Remember, the cultured diet is not man-made. Besides, man shall not live by bread alone but by the living Word of God (Mathew 4:4). Unfortunately for some people, their diet is not quite different from what the world consumes. It is largely made from ingredients produced by popular culture, which is quickly fed via the intentionally well-strategised public relations machine manned by social and mainstream media personalities – the majority of whose agenda is averse to the foundations of the dictates of the culture of the Kingdom. Meanwhile, the meal spread at the multi-star Michelin restaurant known throughout the Kingdom as Prayer, Fasting, and the Word gets pushed back further from our personal dining experience or planned dinner parties.

The importance of learning the Word is highlighted because it is in the absence of this learning that we speak to each other in tones that are unseasoned – no grace is applied. No building up of each other in the most Holy faith. No joy in our ministry, lapse in judgement and difficulty discerning what is of God. Instead, only selective forgiveness and limited compassion are interspersed sparsely with genuine love. Immaturity reigns. No change - the uncultured remains.

Teaching and learning for the standardisation of beliefs and norms – must not only be continuous but should begin as soon as possible. The Word of God is the food that nourishes and feeds the newborn, as instructed by the apostle Peter in his first epistle (1 Peter 2:1). Nothing is more important than being fed the appropriate food early on, strengthening their faith. Understanding the basics forms a firm foundation on which to build, and the likelihood of them behaving contrarily is lessened. By passing on and grasping the knowledge of the birth of the church – its origins - for example, comparisons can be drawn as opportunities are given for people to analyse how far we have deviated or how closely we are aligned.

Christianity is an intellectual discipline. Knowledge of God's word should not cause anyone to feel intellectually inferior. The more learned each person is in the Word of God, the less likely they are to entertain jealousy, envy and deception. A right understanding of the Word leads to an appropriate worldview and the correct church and Kingdom perspective. There is also a noted maturity in an 'educated' individual or congregation. There is wisdom in their words and care in their behaviour.

And that is even in the absence of chronological age. This means it is not only seen in those over their 40s or 50s, etc, but even our young people – people of all ages, tend to demonstrate what is quoted in scripture that the – fear   of the Lord is the beginning of wisdom (Proverbs 9:10). That fear and reverence for God cultivates wisdom as the word of God gives light and understanding to the simple.

Word of caution: too much knowledge can lead to pride. Encourage humility coexisting with knowledge – humility, because we have not yet attained it. Hebrews 13: 14-16 says that here we have no city, but we look for one to come – this world is not our final home, and neither do we have anything permanent here. We must live in that consciousness. Constantly aware of an eternal life to come. The more cognisant we are of that, the closer we are to an understanding of our culture, and living with that hope is a sign of spiritual maturity - because of the realisation that what we have here is nothing in comparison to what we will gain.

Our destiny is at stake, and how we live is not meant to be abstract; all truths must be applied to our lives. God has ordained His church to be His governmental body on earth, to restrain the lawlessness of man, but when the church throws off restraint and becomes lawless – moves away from scriptural teaching, there is nothing left to restrain lawlessness on earth. There are some Christians who happily say, 'this is how I am, don't try to change me – or, 'it is too late for me to change'. But all believers should align their orthodoxy with orthopraxy to achieve the same reference point and the same behaviours.

In that regard, there is no need for anyone to change anyone – but rather, as we adhere to the Word of God, we should see the change in ourselves, and others see it in us also. This is because old things have passed away; behold, you have become new... A new creation, a brand-new man (2nd Corinthians 5:14-21). The end of self-defeating language. Seek daily to walk as a new person, speaking a new language with a new tongue. A new vocabulary – a language pertinent to a cultural identity. Our state of being cultured is never stationary or brought to a standstill, but always seeking to exhibit more of the expected qualities.

The Word of God is characteristically immutable, carrying on affecting generation to generation. Its effect is scalable - going from the individual to the wider church group...whether a small congregation or a megachurch, whole families, or entire communities. It guides our thoughts and language. As we apprehend the truth of the Word through faith, we then have the inner personal experience of that individual relationship and understand how our problems can be solved through the principles outlined in the Word, which enhances the possibility of shared experiences and assumptions.

Beware of Pride

While prayer, fasting and the Word are woven into the very fabric of our cultured selves and are necessary for embedding Kingdom culture, pride is intricately woven into our uncultured behaviours. And that is the other side of the word... it in its negative context. That said, the etymology of pride tells us it is a polysemous word that has evolved over time along with society and culture. It has had several changes in meaning over its lifetime but continues to enjoy the unfortunate position of being the first sin ever to be committed.

The common root word for pride in Hebrew is gaon - [/a"G] and refers to arrogance and insensitivity to the needs of others. Pride is the first sin. It was committed in heaven by an angel, lucifer (Isaiah 14:12-15 and Ezekiel 28:11-19). Because of his beauty and wisdom, he promoted himself and rebelled against God. Repeatedly, he said – "I will". He exalted himself and lost his special privileges and beauty and is now in irreconcilable opposition to God.

The English form of the word found its way into our vocabulary in the 1500s as part of old English. Later, around the 14th century, it is used to refer to someone exhibiting reasonable self-respect. However, it has taken on a few other meanings since the 1970s and possibly not long before. Therefore, it can easily switch from carrying a positive to a negative connotation – however, it is generally easy to identify which meaning is intended.

The biblical definition of pride is "an inordinate love of one's own excellence." There is no law against a healthy love of self and accomplishments, but not to the point where it is idolised – then it is sinful. In fact, Scripture tells us that God opposes and resists the proud but gives grace to the humble (1 Peter 5:5). God is always and will always be condemnatory of pride. It is something God hates and is high on the list of contributing factors to the general and progressive irreversible degeneration of human character.

Throughout the Bible, Pride is singled out as a known engender of God's anger and bring His wrath. It is conceived in the heart of the individual, is antagonistic to Kingdom culture and obstructs it from being embedded. It makes a big contribution to the perilous state of our culture, is the opposite of humility, and is demonstrated with selfish, wicked actions such as tale-bearing and slanderous.

Sometimes difficult to spot, but like jealousy and envy, it eats away like unwelcome yeast in any dough. Pride is having a high opinion of oneself – a feeling that you have more importance than others. For some reason, you should be treated more favourably. Pride is to exalt oneself, which usually gives birth to evil.

It is within the confines of the will that we humble ourselves before the Lord. 1st Peter 5: 5-6 says, "All of you, clothe yourselves with humility toward one another, because God opposes the proud, but shows favour to the humble. Therefore, humble yourselves under God's mighty hand so that He may lift you up in due time."

Pride opposes a healthy, Godly culture.

Every human being, whether a born-again Christian or not yet of the faith, can occupy either a state of pride or humility. And this can occur at any point in life or along the faith journey. No one should consider themselves above being tempted to be proud or falling prey to its force. Hence, the Bible teaches us to – humble ourselves... an action we all must wilfully take daily.

Many times, we pray and ask the Lord to humble us – when he says we are to humble ourselves – He then creates 'humbling' situations or experiences, and we sometimes fail miserably.

Pride is a grave sin and must be removed from the individual. If left unchecked, it destroys relationships, teams, the church, and ultimately the individual. No one is drawn to a prideful person. This can affect the development of relationships and disable or disrupt culture, as it mars assumptions and skews perspective. Over the years and as we interact with society, notably, words such as 'elite' and 'posh' have made their way into church circles, sometimes as a joke, other times mockingly.

In society, however, they have become synonymous with people said to be in society's constructed 'upper class', who are assumed to be in receipt of 'favourable' treatment in various sectors, even in the church - as opposed to other members of society or the congregation. For someone who feels this does not apply to them – it is not how they view themself – it can be hurtful. It implies that the labelled individual is entitled, rude, spoilt, pretentious, desires to be in society's 'upper class', and seeks favourable treatment. I am not sure anyone finds it complimentary to be called proud. Not with all its corresponding negative connotations. Beware, satan would want us to feel 'special' or take it as a status symbol being called any of the variations of pride. But that is a ploy from the enemy – because to embrace that label is a risk that you will be tempted to want to live up to its requirements. All of which are unbecoming of a Christ-centred life.

Be mindful, vocalised labelling, particularly outside of formed connected relationships with mutual understanding and respect, can be viewed by the recipient as unfair or even cruel and lead to a transactional stage 1 relationship only. Similarly, the presence of pride prevents movement to a personalised relationship with genuine friendship and belonging. Neither is conducive to the continuity of a healthy, Godly, psychologically safe environment, which is necessary for culture to form or to be sustained. From the top down and across, widespread mutual respect is paramount and instrumental in bringing people together.

Pride, left unchecked, makes its way to the outside, is displayed in various ways, and can hinder individuals from asking for help or admitting wrong. It affects the way we accept feedback or be corrected. It has a fundamental debilitating effect on how we worship God because it seeks to omit mercy and ignores grace, as its primary goals are to judge others and satisfy the 3 aspects of I -I want, I feel, I think.

It does not attract God's presence. This is because it opposes his instruction to love others and not simply to love but - to love them as ourselves. It also brings with it the need for control which over the years has loomed largely as it has moved the divine mandate to dominate the earth – to be misconstrued with - dominate and control each other. Our responsibilities, as stated in Genesis 1:26 are to rule over the creatures of the earth, fish of the sea and birds of the air and to represent God to the rest of creation, as we have been created in His likeness and very image - which represents Him to what He has created.

It is unwise to seek to dominate as opposed to seek to get to know each other. And this process may take a while longer for some, which can be due to many reasons. By getting to know each other, we are well on our way to breaking down unwarranted assumptions and perceptions to find common ground. God's desire is for fellowship and dependence on Him, which mirrors our fellowship and relationship with each other.

Humility is the only antidote to pride

Before honour is humility – before dishonour or destruction is pride. There are many characteristics of a humble person. For example – we know that a cardinal sign of humility is service. Humble people serve others. Note that service is a deliberate action. Serving is humbling – not just serving the pastor and leadership but seeking to extend that to serve each other. It is an action of the individual's will. Done deliberately until it is done without thinking. It becomes part of the culture.

The desire of a humble person is to be interdependent on each other, as opposed to being independent ... opting to go it alone with the hope of getting all the glory and accolades. Self-seeking actions, such as the above, disconnect us. Humility connects us. Everyone who exalts himself shall be a base, and in Philippians 2, we see where Paul said, therefore... God has highly exalted Christ and given him the name above all other names not because he was his only begotten son but because He – humbled himself.

Isaiah 14:12, Ezekiel 28:16 and Revelation 12:7-9 all tell of the fall of Lucifer when he did the opposite of what Jesus had done. He embarked on an aggressive self-aggrandisement exercise –

driven by unhealthy personal ambition - looking for equality with God and seeking to promote himself. The outcome - he was thrown down.

The humble person is considerate and consciously reflects on their behaviour. They seek to entreat others to come and stay instead of assuming the role of unauthorised gatekeepers blocking the seemingly more gifted or spiritual or...They seek to live peaceably, conscious of the warning that while it is nigh impossible to cause an offence – it is always possible to seek forgiveness and to forgive.

A humble heart guards excitedly their salvation. It recognises and embraces God's mercy, grace, the blood of Jesus, and justification and is gloriously happy to share all these and other divine favours. Humility causes us to be perpetually aware of God's presence and leads us to be accountable to church leadership and each other.

The rule that governs one's length and breadth of influence – is humility vs pride. People in a position of influence within the organisation must exhibit humility through word and deed. Leaders blazing the ethos of humility help to encourage this. And, in a culture where humility is encouraged, there is a celebration of each other's strengths even in the absence of some human-defined greatness being achieved.

Humility	Pride
Humility puts the individual at the front of the queue for Godly promotion and negates envy or jealousy.	Pride reduces and negatively impacts one's breath of influence.
Humility consolidates our culture of love and Godly character.	Pride breathes contemptuous cruelty and hate and inhibits the formation and sustainability of our culture.
Humility is the fundamental characteristic of the – cultured.	Pride is the primary characteristic of the uncultured.

Personal Notes and Reflections

What is mentioned in Chapter 5 that I can relate to?	Is there anything I have observed that I could add?	What are my views on the imperatives?	Any other comments

CHAPTER ` 6

CULTURED

The value of values

"Values are like fingerprints. Nobody's are the same, but you leave 'em all over everything you do." Elvis Presley.

It is customary to see vision, mission and values displayed, providing direction, focus and inspiration to fuel the realisation of shared goals. Combined, they help to guide behaviour and serve as tools that aid the decision-making process.

The mission statement tells the public what we do – who we serve – meaning who we offer 'service' to... and why. Any changes to this can affect the culture.

The vision statement succinctly describes the aspirational state as envisioned by all who are part of its development. The vision should inspire, motivate, and create a sense of excitement for the future. It keeps you en route and lets you know when you have arrived at the desired destination.

Values support the vision and mission of the organisation and describe the culture that will drive the way goals will be realised. They are overarching. The philosophy of the organisation. It is its personality recognised and understood by all. They guide the way congregants interact internally and externally with the community and wider stakeholders. It's the values that define and communicate local culture and beliefs. They are pivotal, particularly during periods of change and are used to encourage or drive performance.

Together with beliefs, shared assumptions, perceptions, traditions, norms, stories, and feelings, they tell the way things really get done. And leaders must be proactive and intentional in shaping them. These are at the core of people staying for the meal or excusing themselves from the dinner table. They create the perception of a safe space, manage the expectations of new members, and enhance engagement. Everyone must know what these values mean and how to apply them to enable internal systems and processes to function optimally.

It is the values that we live by that motivate congregants to tell others about their church. People who do not feel proud of, happy about, or belong to a congregation would quite likely not invite others. Please note, they are not dictates for daily living; neither does a value in isolation create the organisational culture – the set of core values do, but they help us to understand the link between beliefs and actions and are manifested in actions, behaviours, and beliefs. They are important means of communicating how leaders and teams operate, interact and behave.

When there is inconsistency in beliefs and behaviours, an environment of mistrust and hypocrisy is created - having the right behaviours in the presence of misinterpreted beliefs can be a sign of legalism. Values must be in place to connect both.

Having a core values statement is an essential document to encourage the behaviours to create a culture that will serve the vision. Cultural inclinations become well entrenched over time, for good or bad – tended or unintended. The absence of a values statement does not mean the absence of a culture –

culture exists with or without a well-developed or declared value statement. When it is the latter, that can be an indication that the culture was not developed with intentionality around here.

An unintentional culture is synonymous with an unattended environment. Unfortunately, in such an environment, many things are left to grow; inevitably, some things will flourish more than others. This can lead to under or overutilisation of different types of resources with little to no value realised. No benefit to the organisation. The core values guide decisions around priorities and resource use; they help promote the ingredients required to reinforce the strategy and develop a healthy culture.

Every individual and, likewise – every church values something.

This could be from transparency and self-discipline to learning and development, as well as concern about people, the ones in our churches and those in our communities. It may be something about holding a deep-seated sense of pride in the church's history, mission, or vision. It could be that justice and wisdom are valued around here.

It should be that it goes without stating that respect, integrity and moral conduct are valued around here – unfortunately, as more of our culture gets eroded, these are some that could make a big statement and an even bigger impact – if lived out.

Whatever ... the bottom line is, it is helpful for everyone to understand what is valued in your organisation and remember, this is identified from - actions.

Buy-in is necessary for effectiveness. Therefore, once defined by all, the whole team, group, or wider church community must be unified around the agreed set of values. This is opposed to the unattended environment, where they need to be described.

Communicate. Communicate. Communicate.

 Oversharing is welcome, particularly when shaping a new corporate culture. Sharing the core values that current members agreed with helps individuals remember why you do what you do and how they get done. It can be a source of motivation and inspiration. Values should motivate people to act.

A sense of healthy pride in what you are doing as an individual or a congregation reinvigorated by a set of core values can attract new members to the church.

Communication is important as it alerts those who are seeking like-minded believers or a faith community to easily identify with your values and spiritual and social goals, as this may prove attractive to them. Communication is also important for informing the external community of the foundational principles by which the organisation operates.

Values guide our relationships and determine networks. Networking with like-minded people and organisations is an important reflection of your core values. Pre-COVID-19, many churches were well underway with community outreach and post-pandemic, that for some has increased while others are new to this way of doing church. Irrespective of which of these categories your organisation recognises, there is no doubt there are countless opportunities to serve your local community. And no doubt, these are welcome opportunities with possibly limited resources, which restricts capability and makes it impossible to always undertake them all. This decision of what to do and in what order of priority can be made easier by revisiting the core values.

Corporate values communicate authenticity that attracts others and makes your organisation memorable. Therefore, they should not be vague or developed haphazardly. They should be specific and linked to measurable behaviours and activities. (Gleeson B. Forbes Magazine, 2021).

Here are some points to consider in developing your core values:

1. Why does the organisation exist?

2. Be honest about the behaviours you want to guide interactions and completion of tasks.

3. Think about how you want to be thought of by the public

4. Decide how they will be communicated or socialised

5. Publicly share ways that team members have put core values into action to motivate others to do the same.

Remember that values-led leadership and decision-making can be challenging, particularly as we are in an environment of choice; however, it is crucial to guide the necessary internal conduct and the organisation's relationship with the external environment. Core values that are aligned with biblical principles and ingrained can have a positive impact on scalability and growth.

Personal Notes and Reflections

What is mentioned in Chapter 6 that I can relate to?	What do I think about the church having values?	What are my core Values?	Any other comments

CONCLUSION

From secularism to social desirability bias, movement of people, mortality, and other factors – we may never be able to say precisely what are some of the reasons behind the reduction in the size of most of our congregations and the notable shift in our culture. But we can cheer up. The decline in our culture and reduced size of churches should not be treated with a fatalistic shrug – a fait accompli. From history and the testimony of the cultured remnants, we know that The Holy Spirit is integral to resolving church problems, the conviction of leaders and the provision of workers.

While there are many assumptions and anecdotal evidence, the individual context must be analysed if the true causative factor is to be understood for meaningful interventions. A move away from generalisations to a targeted approach demonstrates intentionality and adds value as it speaks to your specific what, why, where, who, when and how.

It also helps to revisit the fundamentals... repentance, prayer fasting and the confession of our faith as we seek to grow and develop.

By looking again at the mode of delivery, content, and possibly frequency with which scripture is taught – with the aim to teach the whole Bible and make its truths and principles central to respective organisations, it gives everyone the same reference point. Together with actions, they are excellent means to delineate sound doctrine and prohibit the spread of falsehood within the organisation, impacting other communities. Truth is enhanced, strengthening the core corporate belief system for clear understanding and unity in cultured practices and behaviours.

An awareness of pride and its consequences is crucial for connectedness and belonging. Seeking to wilfully embrace the opposite – humility - attracts others, encourages service, and builds strong, meaningful bonds.

Our values help to inform our thoughts, words and actions. Where values are valued, people grow and develop as decisions are taken with confidence, goals can be set with clarity and plans executed intentionally.

Adding any of the above and bringing various culture-shaping interventions together can lead to valuable change. Bear in mind that setting the culture should be an early priority—a way to clarify what the possibilities are, even as strategy is being refined. Multinational companies such as Google, Apple, and others have very distinct cultures, and so do ethnic communities, political groups, and countries. Every ministry, working group, committee – team, or church have a certain culture that constitutes the ethos of that specific group or community. And that means the wrong culture may just "happen in the absence of intentionality." The right culture needs to be created, shaped and maintained. And the responsibility for doing so resides with the leader.

Seeking to work within the existing culture is invariably the best approach, as step changes are facilitated in a graduated manner. Systematic, targeted, and integrated cultural interventions, designed around transforming a few critical behaviours at a time, can also energize and engage the most talented people and enable them to collaborate more effectively and efficiently.

Where there is coherence among the culture, strategic intent, and agreed values, the organisation is attractive to current and potential members. Remember, culture develops over time, and a deeply embedded culture will only be changed over time. Developing your culture requires tenacity. Guarding your culture requires discipline.

Coming together as a Christian congregation is not only good for individuals and for guarding our culture, but it is also imperative. Being part of a congregation - a church, does people good. The gospel is good news and will be so eternally. Therefore, this must be said in an age when churchgoing is often depicted as a "quasi-pathological disorder" (borrowed). Which makes the growth and proliferation of local churches something Christians do well to desire passionately.

Therefore, it is unwise to see culture as an excuse or a diversion; instead, it should be seen through the lens of an important means by which people are inspired to connect motivated to serve...grow and develop.

Question – what is your appetite for change?

Post covid – and we see the appetite for those we no longer see in our pews has changed. While we can't definitively say the reasons behind each empty seat at the dining table, neither can we take personal or corporate responsibility for each - we also know that we cannot apathetically meander along. Not if we are to bid wonderers to come – not if we have a heart to see people come to Christ. It is difficult to see how we can continue with business as usual and not capitalise on the opportunity to meaningfully reset both as an individual and as a church.

We have explored how we do church – is it time we explore how we – are as a church?

Printed in Great Britain
by Amazon

45005819R00069